Learning to Balance in a Wobbly World

Matthew Humphreys

Learning to Balance in a Wobbly World

ISBN: 978-1-7385225-6-9

First published in Great Britain
in 2025 through Amazon self-publishing
service Kindle Direct Publishing

Produced in the UK by The Book Writers' Resource
www.tbwr.co.uk

For my amazing family
&
those who have helped me with this book.

Contents

Mum's Foreword

When Matt told me he had started writing his story I was surprised, but I've learned to expect the unexpected from Matt. I mean writing a story of his life so far, when you have dyslexia that has caused problems with school, reading and writing, even before a brain injury, would put most people off. But my middle child is never one to be put off. Our lives changed forever on Halloween 2008, not just for Matt, but for his brother, sister, me, and the extended family. It's an experience I would not wish on anyone, but it's awful to say, if anyone was going to cope, fight, look for the positive out of any situation, and teach us all how much can be achieved, it was Matthew Humphreys. I'm so proud of what he has accomplished, some of the opportunities he's had wouldn't have happened without his brain injury, but Matt would have achieved and strived to get the most out of his life anyway. His disability is cruel, affecting his movement in all areas of his body, causing pain constantly with the dystonia, as well as affecting his speech significantly, without affecting his mind or understanding. Though none of this stops Matt, he used to say, 'if you can't do it one way, try another way'. I hope you enjoy reading his story so far, I'm sure there will be more adventures to come.

Introduction

Written by Melanie Alesbrook, the member of staff who inspired me to write my Life Story and without whom, none of this would have happened.

I first met Matt in December 2022, and all I did was give him the chance to talk and I really listened. I soon realised that he is a very astute young man who often surprised me with what he had to say, and I wanted to know more.

Early on, I remember going to buy a Christmas present with Matt for his sister, a garden ornament Yoda. Matt wanted me to write a message to stick on the bottom, but I couldn't understand what he was telling me. When he typed it into his speech machine it was, "Payback is a bitch!" because he was getting her back for last year's present to him, which was a tiny present but in a massive box. At that stage it surprised me because I didn't expect him to say such a thing; Matt struggles physically with his speech and often requires you to be patient and wait. One of Matt's favourite mantras is, "Don't judge a book by its cover" and he reminded me that this is something we all tend to do.

Another time early on, I remember walking down to the coffee shop with him in his electric wheelchair, and we had to cross the road at the pedestrian crossing. I remarked that he was like Jesus, because all of the cars stopped way before we even got to the crossing, like the parting of the waves. He replied, "Nobody wants to run a little crippled boy over!" with a knowing grin on his face.

I am an English teacher who took early retirement, and I work a few hours a week for an independent living provider for adults with complex needs, such as learning disabilities, autism and physical disabilities like dystonia. I try to make a difference, and in Matt's case that was to encourage him that he had a story to tell, a great "voice" and he should start to write it down. Every word is Matt's. To begin with he'd type a bit then I corrected spelling, worked with the sentences, enhanced punctuation and put it into paragraphs, but every word is Matt's. It's taken us over a year, but as the story grew Matt's writing improved, he enlisted friends to help edit and the final bit of editing he's worked really hard and done mostly himself. But every word is Matt's.

Matt has a dry, sarcastic and sometimes dark South Derbyshire sense of humour and he's actually very funny. He's got an important story to tell in a very engaging 'voice' that is full of charm and sometimes wisdom. I've encouraged him to write it down because I think the story is worth telling, and not everyone always takes the time to listen. It seemed like a mountain to climb at the start Matt, but we did it, one step at a time.

Matthew Humphreys

Learning to balance in a wobbly world

I've sat and contemplated whether to have another whiskey or any more alcohol to drink, but now I'm considering whether or not to write down my thoughts. Some of the things I think, well... let's just say, they're not for the delicate minded.

For example, today I was wondering what would happen if a monkey and a rabbit mated, what would it come out like? Would it hop or walk? Would it swing or leap? And what would it be called – a Rabbey or a Monkit? (Yes, I'm that guy.)

Anyway, I should probably start my story now.

Hi, I'm Matt, I've been told I've got an interesting 'voice' and a story to tell, but I'll let you be the judge of that...

CHAPTER 1

Before everything became fudged-up.

I thought it would be a good idea to start with my childhood, but actually, I don't really remember all that much about it. I think that's something to do with having a brain injury, but I do sort of recall bits and bobs.

You could have called me a bit of a problem child, but in my defence, you should've seen my brother. To be fair, I don't blame him directly for anything, but he is largely responsible for most of the funny events that have occurred in my life. For example, although it's a bit fuzzy, according to my uncle, when I was about three, I was chased around his garden by my brother wielding an axe. In reality, we were only playing and, now

I come to think of it, I do remember hitting my brother so hard with a recently acquired plastic sword that I broke it. So, on second thoughts, maybe I deserved it!

My brother is two years older than me, but we liked to do things together. By way of example, he once took the stabilisers off his bike, and it was only a few hours before I wanted to remove mine too. On reflection, this might not have been such a good idea. My Dad said it was easier to learn how to ride without them, whilst going down a hill. This may have been a good idea if he'd spotted the bush at the bottom of the hill. Unfortunately, this wasn't the case. To cut a long story short, my Dad spent the next ten minutes fishing me out of the shrub, a task during which I wasn't exactly silent. The next day though, I was riding my bicycle unaided, so I'd have to say that it was a success. Sometimes in life, you must fall down to get back up again.

On another memorable occasion, my brother said that he wanted to try snowboarding, so obviously, I wanted to as well. He says I was better than him – I don't really remember much, I just remember him always trying stuff and falling on his arse. He remembers me copying and, although I didn't always do the trick, I stayed on my board most of the time... but I don't think that was always the case. I was only copying him because he used to get so annoyed and I found it hilarious, antagonising my brother, so I kept copying him. It's only brotherly love!

I used to spend most of my weekends playing either or both rugby and football. I was though, if I can say it myself, quite good even though I was one of the smallest in the rugby team. Once again, I started rugby to annoy my brother, but after a while I started to really enjoy myself and loved being in the rucks and scrums, basically in the middle of all the action. Mum used to be scared when everyone would pile on and I would be at the bottom, which was most of the time, and the fact that I was one of the smallest players on the team didn't help make her feel any better. I also played football, but with football I didn't copy my brother. The thing I struggled most with was that I used to have to remember not to use my hands, so I ended up as the goalkeeper, naturally!

Speaking about brotherly love, I should probably mention my sister. She was the tamer one out of the three of us, but I do remember some fun stuff that we did as children. Like riding our duvets down the stairs, pretending we were sledging in the artic on a snow mobile or something – that was until we reached the bottom of course, then we would do it all again. We ruined so many duvets, but somehow, we never got into trouble... maybe it was because she was the youngest, or the fact that my Mum always wanted a girl. Me and my brother still accuse Mum of favouritism!

Me and my brother playing in snow before brain injury.

Me, brother and sister before brain injury.

CHAPTER 2.

The s**t hits the fan.

Okay, now we get to the point in my life where everything changed.

When I was ten years old, I had an accident, the type of accident that messes you up for a while. Yes, this is the point where I have my brain injury. I've said that I was a strange kid, well I used to sleep with my head hanging over the edge of my cabin bed. (For those of you that don't know what a cabin bed is, it's like a bunk bed but without the lower bed.) Anyway, I'm not entirely sure what happened but it was Halloween, around midday, and Mum wondered why I was quiet. When she found me, I was hanging from my cabin bed by my neck. I am lucky because Mum is a trained nurse and has knowledge of CPR – without her I wouldn't be here to tell you, my story. And (not to be big headed) some of the things I've done are quite impressive.

My wonderful, caring brother and sister had Nan looking after them, and they still insisted on her letting them go trick or treating that evening. You've got to love siblings! I just remember waking up in hospital a week later, with a tube sticking out of my throat and attached to a machine that was helping me to breathe. I couldn't talk much, my throat was dry and sore, and I had to learn how to breathe and talk together, because I had a tracheotomy. I lay there confused about what had happened. I could move, but nobody really knew what my injuries were yet. I was transferred from Burton A&E to Stoke hospital, then after a couple of weeks to Derby Hospital.

The first few weeks were alright, it was after a few months when my disability started to change. I have what's called quadriplegic or generalised dystonia, meaning that all four of my limbs won't do what I want. My balance and speech are also affected. I'm constantly in pain with spasms or muscle tightness, but it took a while to set in. So, I was only slowly realising that I could no longer do the things I could do before.

Before, I loved to be active. I played rugby, I swam, I used to run everywhere but most of all I loved to ride my bicycle. Now I could no longer do any of that. I tried not to think about it though. There was one thing I loved to do and that was prove people wrong. After the accident, when I was in a coma, my Mum was told that there wasn't much chance of me doing much of anything. I was sort of expected to be, to put it bluntly, a vegetable.

But did I prove the doctors wrong! And I got such a sense of satisfaction out of it that I continued trying to prove the doctors wrong. I attended the hospital school and with the help of the brilliant OTs, Speech Therapists and Physios at Derby Hospital and with the support of my amazing mother, who stayed with me throughout it all, I learned to walk, talk and (sort of) get back to normal again. Obviously, I would never get fully back, but I think I got pretty close, or as close as my body would let me.

I think I worked with the Physios most days; they would come to my bed, and I would go to the Physio Department. I remember riding a tricycle around the wards and travelling up and down the lift on it too. I remember getting stuck in the lift once when, for some reason, it just stopped working and I had to press the emergency button to get rescued. Speech therapy involved a lot of blowing into things at first to get my breath working properly. I know what it sounds like but get your mind out of the gutter!

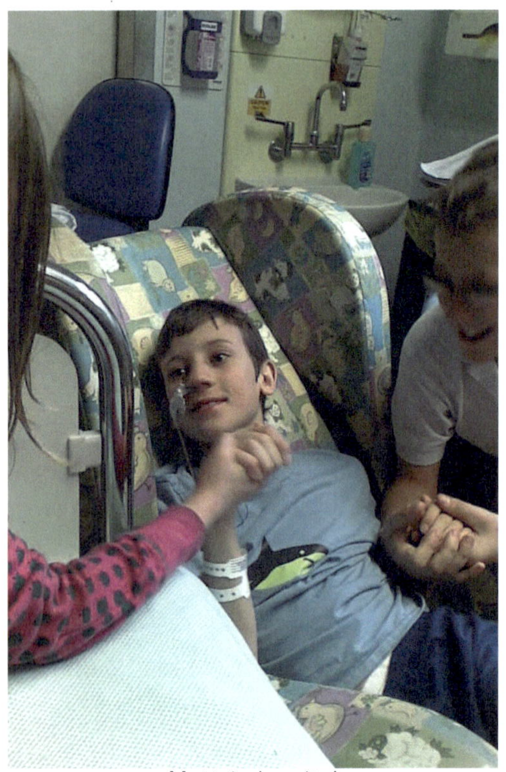
Matt in hospital

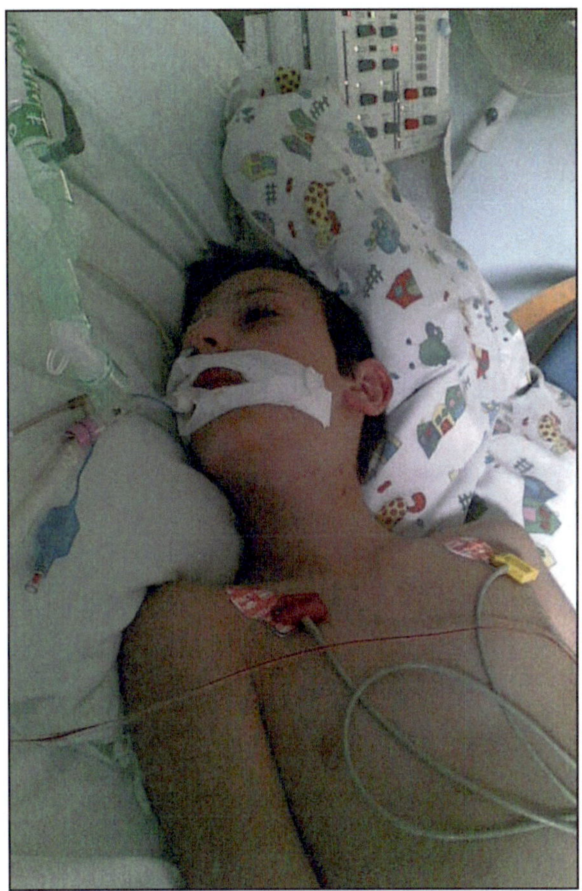

Matt in hospital 2

Chapter 3.

The stuff we have to put up with!

So, I think I was in hospital for about eight or nine months, though I got discharged from the hospital ward after a month on my Nan's 60th birthday. This was thanks to Mum insisting it would be ok, and she would bring me back every day for therapies and reviews. I found out on the day that it was a surprise that I was out of hospital, and therefore I was told to crouch down behind the settee. I mean, I had just come out of hospital, and I was getting shoved behind a sofa! But I love my Nan, so I was happy to do it. I can remember Nan coming into the room and I just wanted to jump out the minute I heard her voice, but I was told to wait. When I did finally jump out, it was just so wonderful. I don't really know how to describe it, but I spent the next ten minutes hugging everyone, especially Nan.

When I first got back home my disability didn't seem too bad, so I thought I could do everything I used to be able to do. Boy was I wrong. Before the accident I was good at swimming, but after I learned the hard way that I was no longer as good as I thought. When Mum took me to the swimming pool I naturally went straight to the deep end and jumped in – but I quickly learnt that this was not a good idea, because instead of swimming I was now more adept at sinking. Mum says I nearly gave the lifeguard heart failure but luckily, like always, Mum was there to save the day.

When I was discharged from hospital, the agreement between Mum and the hospital was that I would go back and attend the hospital school some days and attend my normal Primary School the rest of the time. But I was kind of able to pull a bit of a fast one, because I was only doing half days at my school. Although I loved to learn and I loved being sociable with my old friends, I would get tired very easily. My school was called St Wystans – I know what you're thinking, I'm some kind of posh boy but that's so far from the truth! And honestly, there's nothing wrong with being a bit posh, it just means you talk properly, and you have a bit of money, and that's never a bad thing.

But anyway, I'm getting sidetracked, so on with the story.

Before my accident, I like to think I was one of the top students in my class. This wasn't always the case academically speaking, but it's what I like to believe, and I was quite athletic, so I was good at physical education. But after I got out of hospital, I don't think anyone knew quite what to do with me and I don't blame them. The thing that bothered me is that my friends and everyone else in the school started talking and treating me differently. It was as if they thought I would break if I hurt myself – and I sort of just went along with it.

One time, I remember falling over in the playground and I can just remember everyone around me stopping what they were doing and looking at me, like they were waiting for me to explode or something. Naturally I started to cry. It didn't even hurt that bad, but for some reason I was sitting on the ground bawling my eyes out. Now, looking back on it, I'm embarrassed about how much of an attention seeker I was. I played the part of little disabled boy very well!

Anyway, it was a very good school, and I don't blame them for being a bit apprehensive about letting me back in after my brain injury. I later learned that they don't usually let people who have disabilities in, and I understand why. The building was an old Edwardian building with lots of stairs, so I'm very grateful that they let me back at all.

I wasn't there for long because I was already in my final year when I had my accident, but I do remember my leavers do. All of the Year 6 parents got together and hired a limousine to collect us from the church, where the leavers assembly was, and take us to the pub. Don't worry no underage drinking happened at the pub! There was a bottle of champagne, but me being the upstanding member of society that I am, I did not partake because I was afraid of getting told off by Mum.

The next year I was starting High School, and at first Mum and I went all over looking at potential schools. We went to about five or six different schools but, me being me, I was naturally awkward to place in a category because I was physically disabled but without learning disabilities. Anyway, we found a school that I liked, finally a school where I could have got away with practically anything. I thought it was great but then we got a call from the local High School in my area saying they could have me and naturally it would be a lot cheaper. I was placed in the specialist department of my local Secondary School. I don't want to say that it was rough, but when you put a load of kids with autism and other issues in one place, it is going to be a difficult dynamic.

So, on my first day I quickly learned who

the popular kids were, and I tried to fit in. But obviously they weren't normal popular kids, or at least not what I was used to anyway, so I had to adapt from my old private school ways to a more urban school community. Luckily, I had my older brother who was in another local school, and for some reason he was popular – I don't know how because at home he was a total knob! So, I sort of started imitating him and that was probably not the best idea, because I basically became an annoying little shit – that's all I'm going to say about that part of my life!

I found I could get away with quite a lot at my school at first, but after a while the teachers and teaching assistants kind of clicked onto what I was doing, and I got moved up to the harder classes. I then had my IQ tested. I can't remember the exact score, but I do remember the woman who tested me saying to my Nan and me that it was quite high. From that moment onwards, my plan of just riding the disabled image went to shit. I got moved up to even harder classes with the rest of my peers, and Nan kept asking me about school and giving me random tests about

Me and my sister playing on a slide.

things they didn't even teach in schools anymore. I'm telling you, it was a nightmare, but on the other hand I was able to see some of my old friends from nursery and junior school - basically my friends in the area that I lived.

CHAPTER 4.

Learning to make lemonade when life hands you dodgy lemons.

Another big thing happened around this time – I found an organisation called Cerebral Palsy Sport (CP Sports), or more accurately Mum found them and dragged me along to a few events. Here I eventually realised that the only thing stopping me from doing sport was me being lazy. So, I initially started by throwing a thing called a club. The best way I can describe a club is that it sort of looks like a bowling pin with a weight on the end, and I was kinda good at that, but at one of the CP Sports athletics days, I saw a girl on what was called a Race Runner. But that's not the original thing that attracted me.

The thing that attracted me was that I thought the girl was kinda hot! She offered for me to have a go on her Race Runner, and it felt like I was flying! I could do something that I thought I would never be able to do again, run, and I immediately fell in love with Race Running.

So, obviously, I kept asking Mum for a Race Runner, but at that point I didn't realise how expensive they were. I didn't even know what I was going to do with it, so it took a bit of time before I was able to get one. Eventually, we heard of this charity that helps fundraise for them. Mum got in contact, and they agreed to help me to fund one. When I first got it, I didn't know where to use it, but once I found I could compete on it I was winning every competition I entered...and my success had nothing to do with the fact I was the only Race Runner in England.

It was also around this time that I had finally worn Mum down and convinced her that we needed a dog. So, we picked a dog out of a pen in Derbyshire, but we couldn't take her home yet because she was too young, and we had a holiday planned to somewhere called The Calvert Trust. On the way there we were trying to pick out names, but it wasn't until on the way back that we finally decided on a name. Because we'd had such a good time – climbing up mountains, rock climbing and doing other things that you wouldn't think a disabled person would be able to do – we decided to name the dog after the

Calvert trust. So 'Cally' was our new member of the family.

When we first got Cally home obviously everyone loved her, but there was a slight problem... being a puppy and living on a farm she wasn't toilet trained. So, the first few weeks we came home to presents from her on the floor, and I think you know what I mean by presents. But in case you haven't got a clue what I'm talking about, presents are steaming hot piles of you know what! Obviously, I found it hilarious, but I'm not sure Mum did because she was usually the one cleaning it up.

The whole reason we bought Cally was to help with my walking as I had said that I would take her out for walks like I did with my Nan's dog, Lucy, when she came to stay. I loved taking Lucy out for walks, but with Lucy she was like five-years-old, so she used to walk nicely next to you. Now with Cally, she sort-of did but being a puppy, she would get distracted or scared and try to go in the opposite direction. So, I had to take Mum with me when I wanted to walk Cally, and it was a bit more difficult for Mum to look after me and the dog at the same time, so it worked out that Mum and my brother and sister were taking her out for most of her walks. I was usually left at home while Cally was getting walked, but I was happy because I had discovered films, and my brother had recently set up a Netflix account. At the time Netflix was kind of a new thing, and I was just spending days and days on Netflix watching films. I sort of got a bit obsessed with it, it was all I would do – just lay on my bed watching movies.

Mum tried to get me out of the house socialising with different youth clubs, but they would all end up the same way... I would go for a few months but quickly lose interest. I struggled to relate to the other kids there, but Mum kept finding new ones, again and again, so I pretended to enjoy them because I didn't want to upset Mum. I was a real Mummy's boy in those days, doing everything that she asked although not always at the speed she would like. I would get away with quite a lot because, no matter how naughty I was, I couldn't top my brother. He was in his rebellious phase. So, there was my brother who was the one who was always getting into trouble, then there was me, the disabled one who was trying to live up to my brother but never could. Then there was my sister who was on her way to becoming a professional gymnast – no wonder my sister was the favourite!

Around this time, I was in Year 9 and still competing on the track. One day, I was at a competition and this girl came up to me and Mum asking about the Race Runner and where she could have a go on one. I offered for her to have a go on mine and Mum took over with the rest. Little did I know that in due course she would become one of my closest friends – yes, this was the moment I met Ellie. I didn't know it then, but I would get into all sorts of trouble with Ellie, but not the sort of trouble that you got told off for.

I was doing my mock exams at school at this time, and like every other kid I was a bit stressed. So, I turned to sports and focused all my energy into running on the Race Runner and cycling with my cycling club, Derby Mercury. The only problem was that there were not a lot of disabled people doing cycling at that time. So, Mum took me all over the country to compete but because of the lack of competitors, although I was putting a lot of effort into it, I was struggling to get anything out of it. Eventually, I decided to give it up, not completely but I would put it on the back burner.

Having fun after training session – Sheffield.

Chapter 5

What doesn't knock you down makes you stronger

It was shortly after that I had one of the most memorable and life changing experiences of my life. So, one day Mum got a call to say that my name had been put forward to take part in The One Show Rickshaw Challenge for Children in Need. At first, she didn't tell me because she didn't want me to get my hopes up, but she was asked to take me along to the selection day.

The selection day was what it sounds like... about ten young people who had different life stories, who were there to trial out a load of different activities that we would be doing on the Rickshaw Challenge, but only five of us would actually be chosen. I was told to bring my trike, but what they didn't expect was for me to show up with a racing trike that I had luckily been given a few years earlier by the charity, The Odd Fellows. They had fund-raised for ages to buy it, and it was a thing of beauty – with its slick, white tyres that stood out on the road and its lightened sleek black frame. Not to toot my own horn too much but, my trike was a thing of beauty.

But yet again I'm getting sidetracked and I should be telling you about the trials for the Rickshaw Challenge.

So, there were three main things they were looking for. Firstly, they had us cycling around an old racetrack to see how good we were on the rickshaw. Secondly, we had to carry out different activities to determine how we could work as a team. Thirdly, we were asked to talk about ourselves. I thought that I did okay at the cycling and the speech, but I was a bit worried about the teamwork activities because I was used to working alone. With having done all my athletic and sport stuff, they weren't exactly team-based sports, so it was kind of a new experience. I guess I gave off a pretty chilled out vibe, that was what I was trying to do anyway, I was going for the laid-back approach.

It must have worked, because a few weeks later Mum got another phone call saying I had been picked to take part in The One Show Rickshaw Challenge! I was so excited, but then came the other news – that I couldn't tell anyone. I mean, one of the main reasons why I wanted to take part is so that I could brag to my friends, but I couldn't! I mean, I understand why I couldn't, but I was still disappointed. I had to wait for them to announce it and it seemed like forever until they did, but as a matter of fact it was just a couple of months. The reasoning for this was to help protect me from internet trolls and other unpleasant people, so I didn't mind waiting.

When the day finally came where they were going to announce the participants for the challenge, me and Mum had to travel down to London to meet up with the rest of the team and Matt Baker, who would be doing the challenge with us. Let me tell you something about Matt: he is such a nice guy; he really is just how he comes across on the TV. Alex Jones was nice too, but sadly I didn't get to spend as much time with her over the challenge. The thing I remember most about Alex was getting a big hug from her when I first walked into the studio.

Anyway, once again I'm getting sidetracked.

I think I was talking about the Rickshaw Challenge and going to the BBC TV studios. There was still more waiting for the challenge to start, but at least it wasn't as long as last time, it was only a few weeks. It was finally time to start the challenge, and I was so excited to get started on the rickshaw that my muscles were ready to explode. When it was my turn, everyone said I was going really fast, but I didn't realise. I only realised when I got off the rickshaw because the people who were riding the motorbikes next to me thanked me for letting them go a bit faster than normal because they said they, "got a chance to stretch their legs," – which I didn't really understand because they were on motorbikes!

The next day you would have thought it would be easy with it being the second day, but somehow, I got stuck with a really hilly section. They obviously gave me the hills, because in my story that I'd had to do I had bragged about how sporty I was. Mistake! But I was only trying to get across that however bad you have it, you can do whatever you put your mind to. Also, I think I was kind of the sympathy vote, so they tried to get me on as much as possible.

But I'm getting sidetracked again… we were discussing the hills.

Anyway, they were not small hills, and

I think by my fourth hill my muscles had just about given out. On the one before the final hill, no less. To top it all off, my mate got the big downhill and was named 'Speed Queen.' But then again, somehow, I got away without doing any of the really early morning starts. I'm talking about having to get up at 4:15 in the morning – those got mostly reserved for my mates and fellow team members.

The riding did in fact get easier the further South we got, but the riding was not the bit I was dreading the most – that came next... the speech. I later found out that it would be in front of a fully packed stadium at my local football club, and it turned out that I had good reason to dread it. When I walked out onto the pitch, I totally forgot what I was supposed to say and ended up just saying, "Pardon." Anyway, it was a great game that I got to watch for a change. I'm going to tell you which team I support now, but please don't laugh, it's Derby County. I know they're in a bit of a slump at the moment, but I believe that they will get better soon.

I never knew how often my mind wandered before writing this book, but I am getting sidetracked again!

We were talking about the Rickshaw Challenge, right? So, I made a mess of things, but it was alright as it turns out because the Tannoy wasn't very good, so they ended up using the pre-recorded video of me talking anyway.

The next day was probably one of my favourite days during the challenge, because I got to ride into Nottingham's Ice rink Arena/ Stadium to a full crowd cheering me and Team Rickshaw on. All of my friends and family were there, as well as Torvil and Dean, the Olympic skaters who had trained and came from Nottingham – the feeling was just electric! The following days were great, filled with lots of laughter and good memories, but it was very hard work. I rode into about three more cities along the way but had to change over with the other members of the team when we got close to the centres. I loved riding into the cities because you often had people around cheering you on. I mean, we had that everywhere, but I don't know what it was, you just got a certain sense of accomplishment whenever you were riding somewhere where there were a lot of people.

We were coming to the end of the challenge and as the team were approaching London, when riding into the centre, kids kept jumping in front of the rickshaw, hoping to get on TV. I remember a couple of delinquents that jumped in front of the rickshaw with their bikes, but the assistance riders quickly got them out of the way just in time – they came very close to crashing into me. There was a vote amongst the team to see who would ride the rickshaw to the finish line in the studio and I was voted. This was a huge honour, but I did have to walk the final section because they wouldn't let us ride through the EastEnders set. Anyhow, when we did get through the set, I was chosen to ride onto the stage which was one of the greatest moments of my life!

A few months later I was doing well at Race Running and I was invited to compete at the CPISRA (Cerebral Palsy International Sport and Recreation Association) World Games. CPISRA were a founding member of the Paralympic movement. Originally, I thought it would have been held somewhere nice, like Barcelona or Madrid, but it turns out it was being hosted in Nottingham. To begin with I was disappointed with the location, but then I thought it's still a big deal. When the World Games came around it was not what I was expecting. It was a lot quieter and more organised than I thought it would be. I don't know how to describe it really, I just expected more. At that point, I was one of only a few Race Runners in England – I think there were only four or five of us. I mean, I was no longer the only one, but it had not taken off in the way I thought it would.

So, I was talking about Nottingham. The World Games was a great experience but the bit I remember best is messing around with my mate, Ellie; we were making a train with our wheelchairs and just making fools out of ourselves. I think it was there I started to get feelings for her, but at that period of my life I didn't really know what to do with them. It didn't help that Mum was trying to get me to ask Ellie out. One thing you should know about me is that I will usually do the opposite thing to what people expect from me, and I enjoy making them believe that I'm going to do something and then doing something else completely. Over the next couple of years, I became really good friends with Ellie – in other words I 'friend-zoned' myself.

Anyway, I was telling you about Nottingham. Sidetracked again.

When the games finished, I had come away with four silver medals. It doesn't matter that there were only two people in my discipline, so they were basically medals for losing! But they were medals at the end of the day, something to be proud of. And it meant that I was second best in the world at something – "Take that, doctors!"

I can't remember if it was before or after that when I went over to Denmark for the first time. The main thing I remember is that, at that point in time, I was quite good looking. Well, I thought I was and, evidently, so did some of the foreign athletes. I remember being told by one of the people who worked at the camp that there was this girl who fancied me, but she was too shy to come talk to me. The trouble was, at the time, I used to over think everything, and I couldn't deal with long distance relationships, so I did nothing. Then it just got worse as more girls started coming up to me and introducing themselves. It got to the point that I had to say please stop coming up to me. However, I was sitting with a well-known person at the camp, and the person I said leave me alone to had actually come over to speak to the person with me. I was so embarrassed, and I didn't really know what to say.

Another thing that took me by surprise was the number of people that were in wheelchairs. I'm talking about people that if you saw them on the street, you would automatically think that their legs didn't work, and then here they were running with the aid of the Race Runners. I thought it was amazing that if Race Runners could help them why wasn't it more known about? From that day, on I have always told myself not to judge people by what you think they're able to do. As a result, one of my favourite sayings has been, "don't judge a book by its cover."

BBC Children in Need Rickshaw Challange total money raised.

Me holding a Pudsey bear teddy for Children in Need.

CHAPTER 6.

Stuff it, let's see what happens!

After the Rickshaw Challenge, life, sort of, went back to normal. I say sort of, because I had become more confident, and I was willing to try more things at this point in my life. I was at sixth form and

at first there was a big fuss made over me, and I found, once again, I could get away with practically anything. I got to quite like being on TV, being given awards for Disabled Sports Person of the year in South Derbyshire and Derbyshire, as well as giving speeches to my old schools. But this wouldn't last. I don't really remember much about this period apart from being constantly tired and usually getting into trouble for falling asleep at my desk. The problem was my sleep pattern was out of whack, and I was not sleeping at night when I was supposed to. But anyway, I didn't much see the point in my education at this point and I was mainly focused on my sports and running, which I was doing really well at by the way.

The following year I went back to Denmark but this time with my mates in Team England. I'm going to tell you about my trip to Denmark to compete in the European Race Running Championships. But it's not what happened on the track that I remember about that trip. I went with my friends and fellow teammates Ellie, Rafi and Thomas – at the time I had a massive crush on my best friend, Ellie. We were all staying at this creepy school building in Denmark, attending a training camp. Everyone was having fun during the day, but we were all getting a bit tired of what they were serving for dinner; almost every night it was fish in some weird concoction. By the third or fourth day we were getting really fed up with fish, and on the fourth or fifth day we were given a free day to go around Copenhagen.

Mum said I had to use my semi-electric chair, but let's just say it wasn't the most reliable around the city and I was getting frustrated. Honestly, I was not the nicest person to be around. Then my friend Ellie spotted these little trampolines in the middle of the city and, me being me, I asked if Ellie would like to have a go with me. This would turn out to be one of the funniest and most humiliating parts of the trip and my life. We started to bounce and, at first, it was okay. However, Ellie fell and, as she did, she grabbed hold of the first thing she could... which just so happened to be my trousers. I'd made the mistake of not packing a belt so, inevitably, my trousers came down together with my underwear. I'm not sure who ended up holding the worst end of the stick, me with my trousers and underwear around my ankles, or Ellie being treated to a close-up view of my crotch and arse!

Moments before lost my trousers in Copenhagen – 2nd Denmark trip

So, I was left lying on the ground in the middle of Copenhagen with my trousers around my ankles and my underwear no more than a little higher! My friends and Mum erupted with laughter and, after a while, when I'd gotten over the shock, I joined in too. After Mum had finally gotten around to helping me put my trousers back on and I was sitting in my chair again, I insisted on buying a belt. Fortunately, the rest of the trip wasn't nearly as eventful, and I was lucky enough to come away with a few medals; so yeah, that was my second trip to Denmark!

At school at this time, I was in the sixth form and finding out that I could no longer get away with things that I'd previously been able to. I distinctly remember my IT teacher telling me that if I didn't start paying attention in class, I would eventually be working in a dead-end job. The way he put it was that he thought that everybody would either end up working in a factory or in education. But surely, in the world of the future, jobs in education would be the first to go because machines are more knowledgeable than humans. Consequently, I didn't pay any attention.

At this stage, I thought I was going to be a professional athlete anyway, so what was the point of listening to him? And I was half right. I did make it to a very high level in my sport, although maybe not as high as I'd hoped. So, in a way, I guess my teacher was right but I'm unemployed so f-you sir! Obviously, this isn't something I'm proud of and I do want to find employment, it's just right now I'm focusing on other things.

But I'm getting sidetracked again…

So, anyway, I'm in the sixth form and I'm not getting up to much when, all of a sudden, my

18th birthday rolls around, and what does every young person do on their 18th but drink too much and try to have fun? In my case, though, this was proving to be harder than I thought it would be. The original plan was that we were going to hire a venue, but by then I was using a wheelchair to get around and party venues didn't really do ramps. So, I had the idea of having the party at home. The only problem with this idea was that, while home wasn't exactly small in those days, at the same time it wasn't exactly big. Mum was a single parent raising three children. I don't know how she did it but, somehow, she did. However, I'm getting sidetracked again.

I couldn't have all of my friends come to my 18th birthday party, but I was able to invite Harry, one of my best friends from school. Most of my family also came which was nice, until my Nan decided that I had had too much to drink and started trying to 'help' me. Sadly, my Nan's idea of helping was to try to take my drink off me and get me to go up to bed. Consequently, the rest of the night was fun, wrestling to keep my drink and constantly calling Mum to try and get Nan to stop. Nevertheless, it was a good night.

Not much interesting happened for the next couple of months, other than that I won some awards at the end of the year, and I finished sixth form. Rather than going to university or starting a job, I went to an independent living setting and college for special needs and disabilities in Mansfield, Nottinghamshire. I was finally moving out of Mum's house! But when I did move into the college dorm room, it wasn't quite what I expected. To tell the truth, I didn't really know what to expect but I didn't expect... (how do I put it, so I don't sound like an absolute knob?) well, I was originally put on a corridor with students with very high needs. It was okay because the staff were nice and I was able to have conversations with them and have a laugh, but they weren't always available so, once again, I ended up just sitting in my room watching films.

I was due to start class soon and I was told where to go and everything, but what I wasn't really told is what I'd be doing, and I later found out that was the norm at college. I had gone to college to study sports, but I was quickly learning there was not much structure in sports education, and one of the things I needed was to be told what I'm doing and a little bit of help staying on track. At this time, I didn't really know why I was studying sports – because of my speech, I wasn't the most confident talking in front of large groups of people, so really, I have no idea why I was doing a coaching course.

Originally, I was doing a B-Tec Level One in Sports because I was told it would be mostly on the computer and less talking to people, but that didn't go to plan. Well, I say that because it didn't start until halfway through the year, then I didn't finish it until the next year, so I was put on another course in the meantime, and that was the coaching course. So, I didn't really apply to be placed on the coaching course, I just went with it. But anyway, that's enough moaning. One of the main reasons I chose the college that I was at was the great Physio Department. I loved going down to see the physios, I think it was because they got me doing physical activities and pushed me to my limits, but most of all they were able to have a laugh with me and I felt at ease around them.

At that time in my life, I was kinda going through a weird phase of thinking about the big picture and the meaning of life. Anyway, one day in speech therapy I was going on about finding my place in the world to my speech therapist, and I think she got the wrong idea because she said she's not the right person to be talking about this with and wanted to refer me to the college counsellor. But after I explained that it was just me being weird and going on a mad rant, I think she got the gist of what I was saying. It was just me being me at the time.

I was falling behind with my training, so naturally I wasn't doing so well with my running, and therefore wasn't doing as well with my competing. So, what did I decide to do but start **DRINKING** more with my mates! This was not really a good idea for my mental health, and not just the drinking. It was also the fact I wasn't doing as well on the track. I thought I was in a slump because mainly my disability wasn't getting any better, and my teammates were getting faster, and I wasn't. At the time I felt like I was totally alone but in matter of fact I was just being a whiney bitch because I was focussing too much on myself and not focussing on the bigger picture. Yes, I was getting slower, but I wasn't training as much and my teammates were training hard.

Anyway, a few years went by, and I was at a competition when I bumped into this dead attractive wheelchair athlete, who I'd seen around the track a few times. So anyway, I was a little bit rude to her at the competition – nothing bad, just that she said, "Hi," and I think I just walked by. After the competition I wanted to apologise and tell her that I was in competition mode; competition mode is where I used to just focus on competing and not much else. Anyway, after the competition I felt I needed to apologise so I found her on social media and got talking to her, and before you knew it, I was in a relationship with her. Well, I say relationship but there was one problem – we lived at opposite ends of the country.

So, it was that time again, another CPISRA World Games came around and finally it was somewhere hot – Barcelona, where I learned that Barcelona isn't a part of Spain anymore, but don't take my word for it because I'm not really sure how it works. Mum had rented a villa just outside of the city, the only problem was that it was on the side of a hill so wasn't very disability friendly. I mean, it was a beautiful place but there were just lots of stairs. I remember getting told off halfway around Barcelona for not having any sun cream on but, in my defence, my Nan was giving the sun cream out downstairs, and I was told I wasn't allowed to go downstairs without someone with me. Because everyone was rushing for some reason, I ended up being left out of getting the sun cream, but I'm not holding on to a grudge or anything.

A few days later I was moving into the athlete's hotel so obviously I was excited, but what I didn't account for was my Nan taking half of my money. I was furious because I'd had to save up for ages to get that money and Nan just took it because I apparently had too much. I mean I was angry, but Nan is one of those really annoying people who you can't stay angry with for long, and there was the fact that she is my Nan, and I love her.

So anyway, I was in the hotel and things were going well. I'd settled in alright, but I kept breaking my bed and (not in that way) I was on a pull-out bed – every time I sat down a slat would break. The reason I was on the pull-out bed is that both of my roommates were over six foot tall, so I said I would go on the pull-out bed. My roommates were so nice – Leo, and I want to say Josh. I loved my time at the World Games. Anyhow, the competition started, and I did well, but this was the point I really started to dislike competing. Don't get me wrong, I loved the social aspect, I just didn't like competing anymore.

Anyway, I'm getting sidetracked again.

The first race was the 800 metres, and I didn't really want to do it, but I did because there weren't enough participants, so I stepped in. But it was the next race that I remember the most. The next race was the 100 metres, and the reason I remember it well is because my mate, and main competition at the time, was in it, Gavin. I remember I had a really good start, and I was in for a medal, but then at about 95 metres Gavin flipped his Race Runner right into my lane, causing me to brake and go out of lane. At that point I was behind him, and I still would have won a silver medal, however, unfortunately Rafi was behind me and overtook me when I slowed down for Gavin. I didn't really mind because Gavin is a good friend and I had already said it was going to be my last games, so I wasn't really aiming to medal. Although I did at the 400 metres because Gavin wasn't there – I only had Rafi to worry about. To be honest, I wasn't expecting to beat him, but I had a good plan, and I executed it to perfection.

My plan was to stay with Rafi for 300 metres and then absolutely bomb it the last 100 metres. Anyway, the plan worked, I ended up getting a gold medal!

So, that was the end of the competing for me, but it wasn't the end of the trip so all of team England decided to have a drink together. I just remember getting Leo to do some lunges in these very small running shorts for a dare. To make matters better, I was sitting on a table with all of the coaches, and it was right next to where I got Leo to do the lunges. I looked over at the coaches and their faces were a picture. I mean, try to imagine the look of shock, disgust and then finally laughter at the same time and then times it by four coaches. Anyway, it was a hilarious sight to behold.

Me, my brother and my sister.

CHAPTER 7.

Hey Ho, that's how life goes

I said that I was going to be stopping competing, but I was quick to learn it wasn't that easy, because I was one of the original Race Runners. Race Running had now changed its name to Frame Running. I thought this was so stupid because they only did it to better the sports chances of getting into the Paralympics, but it hasn't gotten any closer, even now. If I had it my way, I would have left competing behind. It was no longer enjoyable to me, but somehow, I kept getting pulled into competition after competition. I mean I was still sort of enjoying the social side of them, but I found with each competition, I was enjoying it less and less.

One day I was thinking how could I stay doing Frame Running but stop competing? It then hit me – I was good at long distance on the track, and I had the mad idea of running a half marathon. However, there was a slight problem. There was only one other person doing it at the time and she was the mother of another athlete, so I couldn't really get advice from her, and there was also the fact that I didn't really know her. But this wasn't going to stop me, and Mum saw that CP Sport were looking for people to do the Manchester Half Marathon, so I thought to myself, 'why not?' I told Mum to get in touch and see if they would like me to enter and raise money for them, but it didn't go exactly to plan.

I was mainly training on the track, that was what I was used to, and that was the problem. A track is flat, and I was to later find out that Manchester wasn't going to be as easy as I expected. In fact, at one point I thought I wasn't going to finish because the pain between my legs from being on the saddle for so long was excruciating. Although I managed a good time for my first half marathon, I said to myself never again! I was ready to give in and hang up my trainers, but then people started congratulating me and I got such a sense of achievement that I knew I couldn't give it up. So, I did another, and another one until I started to enjoy it. My favourite half marathon was around Silverstone racecourse and to this day it's still my fastest time (1 hour 46 minutes) and my favourite race.

It was now 2019, and shit was about to hit the fan. I was planning my next big challenge when I saw that there was this new virus going around and people were starting to get very sick. I live in the heart of England surrounded by farms, so at first nobody really paid much attention. It was mostly in the cities, and, at the time, I was living in Mansfield, surrounded with countryside. As a matter of fact, Mansfield is less than ten miles away from Nottingham, but anyway I was in hospital for the first half of the first lockdown, and then I had to quarantine at Mum's house for a couple of weeks before I could return to college. At that point I had just started seeing this girl at college so I was constantly asking when I could go back to college, and I think this started to annoy Mum. But I'm a man, and I have certain needs. Oh yes, I'm talking about those needs!

But once again I'm getting sidetracked...

So, I was telling you about lockdown, right? Well, when we first went into lockdown at the beginning of the pandemic, I was due to go into hospital for surgery, but that didn't happen until halfway through lockdown. One day I got a call from Mum asking if I wanted to go into hospital; because at this time, people were saying stay away because Corona Virus was everywhere, especially in hospitals, and I didn't really want to die. But somehow, they had managed to keep it mostly out of Oxford, so I decided to risk it and have the surgery – I thought at that time, I would really benefit from it. I have something called a DBS (or Deep Brain Stimulator.) I originally had it fitted when I was thirteen and for the first few years it was great but after a time, I wasn't sure if it was doing anything. I thought it was a good idea to replace the battery in my chest (oh yeah, I am basically a cyborg, but I don't shoot lasers out of my eyes or anything cool like that!)

During this time, I was living away from home at college, and I had just started a new relationship with a girl from college, but what I didn't realise is that after I went into hospital, I would have to self-isolate at home for three months. The surgery went well, and I didn't catch Corona Virus. Win! I returned home which was not where I really wanted to be. I wanted to be at college doing things with my girlfriend and chilling with my mates, but I was stuck at home with Mum. I was, however, able to video chat with my mates and my girlfriend who was something like sixty miles away.

After what felt like forever, but in matter of fact was only a few months, I was finally able to go back to college. It was just in time for my best mate's birthday, and I said I would plan the party.

So, obviously there was a lot of drinking, and some other dumb stuff happened, like borrowing a couple of dresses from a girl that lived down the corridor and then putting them on – for one night, and one night only, 'Matthewina' and 'Louise' came out. I think I remember shaving my legs as well for a laugh, but by morning I wasn't laughing because my legs were red and sore. My skills with my shaver were apparently lacking, or it might have had something to do with the fact that I'd had so much to drink and could no longer hold the razor straight.

Wait, I think I'm forgetting something big that happened before this.

I remember I was telling you about how I had the aim to do a marathon and become the first person in the world to complete one. Well, before lockdown, I entered the London Marathon with SCOPE, which was due to take place early 2020. Mum had to write loads of reports, proving I would be safe to compete in a London Marathon, which was crazy as by then I had already completed six half marathons, without injuring anyone (that I know about.) I know the paperwork was because they didn't know what a Frame Runner was, or how it fitted in. I wasn't using a wheelchair, and I wasn't running in a costume – I needed my Frame Runner to run without falling on my face. Eventually I was approved, and I took part in meetings with SCOPE alongside the other runners taking part that year for the charity. It all felt like it was going to happen, but it then got cancelled because of Covid. What they did instead was hold a virtual marathon later in the year. I know what you're thinking, how can you do a virtual marathon? It wasn't with a VR headset like I thought it would be, because virtual to me meant VR. Instead, you basically did a marathon wherever you could, just as long as you did the distance of a marathon, 26.2 miles.

I chose to do it at Holme Pierpoint in Nottingham because, at the time, I was doing most of my training there. It was flat, so I thought that would help – and I think it would have if it hadn't had been for the wind. I got there and instantly you could feel the wind trying to blow you back, but luckily, I had an amazing team who turned out to support me, consisting of my friends and family. They were all a great help at both motivating and just generally keeping me going. This included refilling me with energy drinks and protein bars like flapjack, and some even brought bikes and rode or ran with me for a lap or something. When I was finally finished, I felt like death, but with the help of my amazing friends and family I was able to set a new world record! It was a lot harder than I expected but I was happy with the time 4 hours 30 minutes.

But anyway, we were talking about college.

When I did finally get back to college, and after the drunken night I was telling you about, Louie went home for the rest of lockdown, leaving me with not a lot to do. But then I remembered I had a girlfriend who lived down the hall, so for the next few months, and then into the next lockdown, I basically lived in her room. I won't tell you what we were getting up to because you can probably guess.

It was getting towards Christmas, and things were starting to open back up again, and I had just started a new course the year before. At first, I was really enjoying it, but when I came back, I don't quite know what it was, but all of a sudden it was not so enjoyable. That may have had something to do with the fact that my disability was getting worse, or maybe it was the fact that my girlfriend was texting me every two minutes and some of the things she was sending... well, let's just say I didn't want my teachers to see.

As I have mentioned, my college was in Mansfield, which is in the countryside, but the course that I had started back at was in the centre of Nottingham. So, I had to get the bus into Nottingham quite a lot, and getting a wheelchair onto a bus isn't always the easiest thing in the world. I think most wheelchair users at some point have come across the arsehole on the bus that, for some reason, is in a massive hurry. For me, it wasn't the first time I had come across someone like this, but one day coming back from class, we were getting on the bus and a dickhead said something like, "I'm getting old here," not having seen me.

My teacher, who was standing behind me, moved back and said something in response like, "He's in a wheelchair, give him some time!" which immediately shut the guy up, but it also annoyed me a bit because he did have a point, I was probably taking a bit longer than I should have. The thing about me is that I believe that we won't get anywhere if we are constantly having other people making excuses for us, and I would have rather her let me apologise and then get on with my day. If we had done that, it would have probably made him feel like even more of a knobhead than he probably did already, and hopefully he would also realise that rushing around like an idiot doesn't always mean that you get anywhere faster.

But anyway, I'm getting sidetracked once again.

So, I was talking about my college course; I was struggling to see the point in it. Actually, I was struggling to see the point in a lot of things at that time, but that might have something to do with going into another lockdown and I wasn't training for anything. With me it's important that I'm doing something to keep my mind off how shitty my life is or was at the time. At that point

I think the only thing that was keeping me going was spending time with my girlfriend. I know it probably wasn't the healthiest relationship, but we made it work until we didn't, or better yet, I didn't.

Let me tell you about New Year's Eve. We broke up on New Year's Eve, or rather I broke up with her. She says it was to do with the fact that she decided to shave her head, but really, it was to do with my own issues – like the fact that my disability was getting worse again and I wasn't in what you would call a good place. So, a few months later I decided to drop out of college. At that time, I was having mixed up feelings about another girl – Ellie. As a matter of fact, some might even have called it love, but I'm not that naïve and I had just gotten out of a relationship, so I wasn't thinking straight. I was also kinda talking to this other girl who I met via this charity I am an ambassador for, called 'CP Teens.' I was sort of being pushed into asking her out by my friends and, don't get me wrong, she was an extremely attractive girl, but I met this girl through Ellie, and something didn't feel right at first. But over time, I did kind of develop a little crush on this girl, well I should probably say woman because at this point, we were about 21. I asked her out on a date, but as usual something got in the way. Unfortunately, we were about to go into another lockdown. Just my luck.

So, I decided to drop out of college and return home a few months later. I don't know if this was the best idea because we were just about to go into another lockdown for the third or fourth time -honestly it was getting hard to keep up with it. At this point I had lost track of what was going on in the world, because all that you saw on the news was that the death rate was going up again and I found it depressing. So, instead of watching the news and things like that, I preferred to watch anything else, which included a lot of junk TV and TikTok videos.

Thankfully, when we were coming to the end of that lockdown, I was able to start running again and I found that Derbyshire had some really good cycling trails that were perfect for my frame. So, with the help of my PAs, I was able to go to a lot of them, but there was an issue with one of my PAs, Sam. He was my brother's best mate and had known me for a while, and the thing that I found difficult is the fact that he would compare me to my brother, and I don't think he saw me as his employer. I had to keep him around because at that time my new step-grandfather was living with us and Sam got on well with him. Mum had just got married again and I liked Dave (my new stepdad), which was kind of confusing. The man that I refer to as 'Dad' is not actually my dad, biologically speaking. But in every other way he is my dad. He raised me, fed me and helped pay for my education and that, so he is my dad. My real dad walked out or something when

I was little, but at least I got some good grandparents out of him.

Anyway, what was I talking about before I got sidetracked again?

Oh yeah, Sam and Ray, my step-Grandad. So, it didn't really work out with Sam, and I nearly gave up running because of him. Well, it was not entirely Sam's fault, but all we seemed to be doing was going for runs and travelling quite a way, and I was not in a good place mentally or physically. But luckily, I was able to employ other PAs: Ross, Adam and Carl. I did get on with them all and Carl was my PA from college, so I had a really good relationship with him. Honestly, he was more like a brother figure than a PA, and Ross and Adam were like mates. But let me say this about Sam, I don't think I would have been able to complete the London Marathon without him – the actual London Marathon in London! Actually, I wouldn't have been able to complete it without any of them, but Sam took me out to train the most.

Denmark at the European Frame Running Championship.

Drunken night with Louie{college}

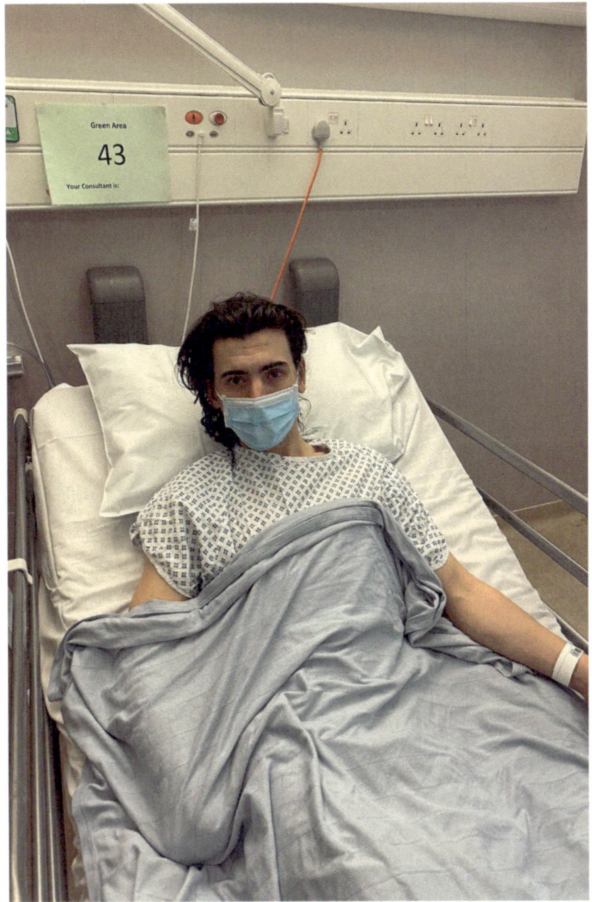

In hospital before I decided to cut all of my hair off.

CHAPTER 8.

Don't judge a book by its cover,
it might surprise you.

In 2021, I did the London Marathon and became the first person in the world to complete the London Marathon on a Frame Runner and, let me tell you now, it was not easy. Have you ever heard of the runner's wall? It's the point in the race where everything starts to hurt, and it becomes really hard to go on any further. Well, I hit my wall at around about the two-mile point of the marathon and if it hadn't been for the crowds and the amazing people of London behind me, I don't think I would have been able to finish it and fulfil my fundraising pledge to **SCOPE** or get my world record.

What can I say about running the London Marathon, other than wow, what an experience! I know no one, even Mum, thought it would be something I could do. But like I said before, one of my favourite things to do is prove people wrong. I have run in loads of races, 5K, 10K, half marathons, but nothing has come close to the London marathon. The number of people, the area it covered, and even trying to get just to the start took ages. The number of positive comments I got from both runners and spectators was amazing.

The start in the holding pens were set out for hundreds of people and depended on your predicted times. The number of people that came up to ask what my frame was and find out about it, as they obviously realised the rough time I was predicted to complete the marathon in was fast. There weren't any runners in costumes in my pen, though I met and bumped into some during the course of the marathon. Or should I say, a huge coffee cup and the runner inside either ran into me, or me into them – we both survived and finished the race!

I was supposed to stop to talk to a reporter on the route, but by the time I saw them I had already passed, and I couldn't get back to them due to the flow of runners. Mum had to keep zigzagging across London to try to see me, but I often didn't see her, as so many people were shouting, "Well done Matt!" I didn't always know that some of the time it was Mum. Although when I got lots of, "You're an inspiration Matt!" I knew that wouldn't be Mum, she would have been the one shouting, "Just use both legs and keep going!" I didn't really look at the sights of London as I was running, I was too busy trying not to crash into anyone, as the race was busier than any other I had taken part in.

After the London marathon I felt like death, to put it bluntly, but I knew that I had accomplished something. However, it was not until we had reached a little pub in the centre of London that my Auntie Jenny found, that I began to feel good. Me, my cousin Joseph and his girlfriend, my second cousin Helen, my uncle Stephen, Auntie Jenny and Mum all crammed into this little pub, and I can just remember having the most satisfying pint, probably of my life.

It was around this time that I got some bad news – my paternal Grandad had died. Although I didn't get to see him much because he lived in Wales and I live in Derbyshire, England, both my brother and I felt an enormous loss because my Grandad was one of those people who you wanted to be around, if you know what I mean. He had a presence as soon as he walked in a room and you just felt safe and happy around him, and you were always guaranteed to get a story about some famous person he had met. When I was younger, he had told me that we were related to a very famous gangster, but I didn't really believe him at first. My brother looked into it though and it turns out that we are in fact related to Murray Humphreys – a very famous gangster from Chicago.

Anyway, I'm getting sidetracked again…

So, it was time to go up to Wales for the funeral, and it was an emotional day to say the least. My brother was asked to sing one of my Grandad's favourite songs which was, What Colour is the Wind? originally sung and performed by Charlie Landsbough, but my brother had been asked to perform it because my brother is a talented musician. You could see he was fighting back tears, and it was a good song. Overall, it was a nice ceremony.

I didn't really do much over the next couple of months. Saying that, I did go to a lot of my brother's gigs. I did say that my brother is a talented musician, but what I didn't enjoy was him rehearsing at 7 o'clock in the morning! I get that he had to rehearse but sometimes I wanted to go down there with a pair of scissors and cut the strings on his guitar – but I would probably end up going back to bed with a black eye or something. But then he would bring me along with him to his gigs and I would be glad he rehearsed because he is a really talented singer. At that time, I was sort of looking for a job or something to do and I was sort of realising my

IT teacher was right – I probably should have tried harder in school. I was really struggling with spasms and my body. At this point in my life, I was living at home with Mum and, to put it bluntly, Mum was getting tired of me sitting around the house being lazy.

It was around this point that Sam, my PA at the time, was leaving me for his dream job in the police. So, my Mum and I had to start looking for a new PA and this is the point I met my current PA and my really good mate, Steve. I was a bit apprehensive at first because Steve is quite a bit older, and he has a family of his own. I tested him out by having him drive me to the Great Birmingham Half Marathon, and on the way, I found out that he had a similar sense of humour, and he was okay with my dog, Charlie. We think Charlie was mistreated as a puppy, so naturally Charlie has some issues. The first time I met Steve, someone let Charlie out, and Charlie went to attack Steve, but to everyone's surprise, Steve didn't react like most people would have done. Don't get me wrong, Charlie isn't a big dog but when you see any dog running at you, I think the normal reaction is to panic. But here was this guy who stayed calm and, by the end of the interview, had Charlie sitting on his lap cuddling up to him. I was very impressed and a bit gobsmacked!

But anyway, I'm getting sidetracked

again.

I was talking about the Great Birmingham Run or half marathon. Well, let me tell you something, I had done a lot of half marathons but never anything as hilly as Birmingham. The people that live in Birmingham are great. The amount of support and motivation I got from the crowds was just unbelievable, I can't tell you the number of positive comments I got from the crowd and the other runners.

Anyway, going back to wanting to get a job, I think one of the main reasons why I wanted to find work at this time was because I was really lonely and wanted a group of friends around me. Well, really, I just mainly wanted a girlfriend, but I figured if I had a group of friends, hopefully they could possibly help me and even introduce me to girls. I wasn't having much luck on the dating apps, but I don't blame the girls. My opening line was a bit dubious and not everyone gets my sense of humour. At that time, I was kind of a loner. Not by choice, it was just that I wasn't really getting out much, so I wasn't making friends. I was so lonely that I started talking to my ex. Although just about everyone in my family was telling me not to, I thought it was my life, I would do what I wanted, and I didn't see the problem with it. I thought my ex was a really nice person, but I later found out the problem was I was getting too attached to her life and what was going on with her. I mean we were still really good friends, and I supported her with some issues she was going through. I'm not going to tell you what they were because they are personal, and I think that would be crossing a line.

After London Marathon with family.

Chapter 9.

Independence at last.

At this point in my life, I was kinda getting fed up with living with Mum, and then my social worker told me about this opportunity to possibly move into a supported living accommodation. Obviously, I jumped at the opportunity and got myself on the list, with Mum's help of course. I was then asked to speak at a corporate event for the company that would be handling my care at the new building. I later found out that it was the 30th Birthday celebration for the organisation (Real Life Options), so it was a good opportunity to get in good with the management side of the company. If I did or said something that could perhaps get me in trouble at a later date, I would have less chance of getting kicked out.

Let me reiterate, by asking me to give a speech they didn't expect me to speak it myself. That would be a laugh – why not get the guy with the speech impairment and stick him up on stage in front of 100 people and expect him to miraculously talk! No, I typed it out on my iPad and then this talked for me. Anyway, I had a few months to write it, so I would write a bit, go back and change it, write a bit more, go back and change what I had written, and so on and so forth. You get the picture. But every time I changed it, I would basically write a new speech. In the end, I just sort of got something down and then forgot about it. I wasn't totally happy with the end result, I could have changed a few things, but I was fed up with editing it and I think the speech was a success anyway – the room full of over 100 people I didn't know were laughing, crying and applauding more than I ever expected. I did get the directors to get the manager of my future home to say yes to a bar or drinks area, even before I moved in but unfortunately, this didn't happen!

At this time, I was still waiting to move in. What I hadn't understood from my social worker and the lady from the supported living accommodation, Amanda, is how long it would take to build the facility. They were still building it, although not from scratch. They (the builders) were converting an old factory and turning it into apartments. So, at this point it was still being built and my moving date kept getting pushed back; first it was April then it got pushed back to May, September and so on and so on. I finally moved in on the 21st of November, 2022. At first it was strange not having Mum around, but after a while I got used to it and I began to settle in. The staff at the home are really nice and good to have banter with. I moved in just before Christmas and at that point there were not many other people moved in and, to tell you the truth, I was getting a bit bored.

I think it was around this time that one of the staff started to say I should start writing a book because, to put in her words, I'd lived an interesting life, I had a lot to say, and I had a good 'voice.' When I talked with her, some of the things that came out of my mouth, well let me put it this way, it's not what she thought I would be saying. The first time I met her I said something like, "I'm just contemplating whether to have a whiskey or not." I was just wondering if it was the right time of day to have a whiskey or too early. She couldn't understand me because she was still getting used to my speech impairment, and it wasn't what she was expecting me to say. I'll give her this, I'm not like other disabled people but, saying that what is 'normal'? Who decided what's normal for a person who has had a brain injury? What I've discovered over the past few years is, there are never two of us (disabled people) who are exactly the same. Actually, scrap that, there are no two people who are exactly the same. I think I'm quite unique if we're being honest. Yeah, it might sound a bit big headed, but I'm one of a kind – there's only one Matthew Humphreys!

But once again I'm getting sidetracked.

So, I think we were talking about the fact that a staff member wanted me to write a book, but at that time I was doing quite a lot. I was trying to write another speech for this charity ball that was coming, I was trying to sort out my bills, which you'd think would be easy – but let me tell you something, it was not! At first the electricity companies said we didn't exist and then we were waiting for a letter that didn't come because we were having issues with the postcode as it was a new build. Thank God I had the staff who worked at my home, especially one staff member, Bev, who had a similar sense of humour to me, so this meant I could have jokes with them. After a while I sort of got tired of waiting for the electric company to get their shit together and I started work on the book.

I was talking about how I had been asked to write a speech for this charity event that I was asked to speak at. Now that I think about it, this probably happened at a different time, but I think it's important so I'm going to carry on talking about it. So, I told you about Ellie earlier on. Ellie set up the charity, CP Teens, in 2013 and although I don't have CP (Cerebral Palsy) I was asked to be an ambassador for the charity when I was about 14/15 years old. Well, this was the time I had a crush on Ellie, so obviously I said yes and ever since then I've not really known what an ambassador does. I was asked to speak because Ellie had seen a copy of the speech that I did at the Real-Life Options event and she thought it was funny, so she asked me to write a speech for the CP Teens ball. The ball is an annual event that CP Teens puts on, and it was the highlight of the year for me because it usually involved a lot of drinking and other fun stuff, like an auction to raise funds for CP Teens. Ellie asked me to make it as funny as the last speech I did but only gave me a 10-minute time slot. Anyone who has ever written a speech knows it is really hard to get it under 15 minutes, but in the end, it was a good speech and, better yet, I didn't have to buy my drinks afterwards! As I had mentioned my time at college and getting drunk on the first night, naturally I think people were trying to see if I would re-enact the funny things I did. But as Aslan says in the film and book The Chronicles of Narnia: Prince Caspian, things never happen the same way twice. I know I'm referencing a kid's book and film but there's something you need to know about me, I love a good reference, and you've got to love Narnia.

Anyway, I'm getting totally off topic. I was telling you I had just moved in, I was having-trouble with my bills, and I was just getting started on this book. So, I am really bad at English and grammar, but the member of staff who suggested the book told me she used to teach English and would help to edit. At this point I had also been asked to do a speech at the official opening for the home. I sort of remember being asked when I had only just moved in, around Christmas, but what I wasn't told is what I was going to talk about. I wasn't told that until about two weeks before the event. I was supposed to talk about how moving in was and what I thought of Real Life Options, so I quickly put together a speech in the fastest time I'd ever done. Obviously, I said the usual about how much my life had changed and that sort of thing, but I also put about the time I'd had a drink with a fellow tenant and ended up over the toilet to get a few laughs. Also, I felt I needed to apologise to the member of staff who was on duty that night and say thank you for cleaning me up, but everybody seemed to enjoy my speech and found it amusing.

Shortly after moving into my flat, I decided to have a housewarming, and I invited friends and family. Unfortunately, a lot of my friends were busy doing other things, so it turned out to be mainly my family and Steve and his wife. The party was actually alright, mainly due to Steve's wife (Mandy) bringing a whiskey cake – or rather a cake made to look like a whiskey barrel in case you were wondering. Yes, I have a bit of an obsession with whiskey! Well, I don't really know if it's an obsession, but I like it a lot to put it bluntly. I have more than one cabinet full of scotch. Anyway, so the party was good, and I enjoyed myself. Soon after the party I was going into hospital for (I can't remember if it was the pre op or the operation) to have the DBS leads taken out of my head, but anyway I was back in hospital again. It turned out that the DBS was doing something, perhaps not much but something. So, after a while without them, I wanted them put back in, because I think everyone could see I was more dystonic and I was suffering with more spasms, and let me tell you something, a spasm isn't a nice feeling. It feels like you're getting stabbed with a hundred needles, contorting and moving.

I don't know why I did this again, but I entered The Great Birmingham Half Marathon. I decided to try and raise some money for this charity that I became a part of called the Silver Lining Brain Injury Charity. They helped me, particularly during lockdown, by giving me something to look forward to and by giving me a community when you couldn't go out. I don't think people realise how important it is to just have someone to talk to.

But once again I'm getting sidetracked...

I was talking about why I entered the Great Birmingham Half Marathon after I found it so hard the last time. Yes, they had slightly changed the course from the last year, but this only by-passes a couple of hills, so it wasn't quite as difficult, but it still felt tiring. Although, saying that, there's nothing like that feeling you get when you finish – it's immense.

I was having more pain now that the DBS leads were out, so first I went back to Oxford and told the doctors and nurses what I was experiencing, and they said I could have the leads back in. I think they kind of new this sort of thing could happen, so they already had a solution for what to do. I would have a DBS fitted again, but a different model that has more capabilities. The way they put it was, like moving from an old Nokia flip up to something modern and new like an iPhone or some other smart phone.

So, the day finally came when they (the doctors) were going to fit it. It was about November time, and they told me the recovery would be easier. I'm not really sure what I did leading up to the operation except get my hair cut – after you've let your hair grow to a certain length, you kind of get attached to it. I know you're probably thinking he's talking out of his arse or I'm some sort of hippie, but getting my hair cut hurt. Not in the physical way, but in the way that you think you're missing something every time you move around. It had taken me so long to grow and I'm not going to say it was like losing a limb because I think that's going a bit too far. I have huge respect for those people who have lost limbs and are just getting on with their lives, but now I feel like I am digging myself a hole. So anyway, digging some more, I had grown accustomed to the feeling of having my hair the way I liked it and losing it was like losing a part of me.

However, when I did finally have the surgery, the surgeon actually thanked me afterwards for making it easier by having a really short haircut. That made the decision to cut off pretty much all of my hair almost worth it. They said that I'd got to let my head heal a bit, so they asked me to come back in a few weeks for the turning on of the DBS. I couldn't wait to see the effect because, at this point in my life, things were pretty bad. The time finally came to turn it on (the DBS) and, in comparison to the old system I had, it was so much better. I could actually feel it, and in the appointment, I had some strange sensations in my body that I had never felt before. I don't quite know how to put it, but it was like a running sensation in my limbs. I think the DBS was working and it was about a week later that I was in my idea of heaven.

I mentioned that I was a big fan of whiskey.

I was on my dream weekend up in Scotland visiting about five different whiskey distilleries and spending too much money. When I was done in Scotland, I was signed up for an outwards bounds holiday in the Lake District for people with disabilities doing things that you wouldn't normally imagine we could do, like caving, zip-wire and there was even an indoor climbing wall. But my favourite activity was the crate building, where the object was to stack as many milk crates as possible on top of each other without falling off. Obviously, we were on harnesses, but at this time I was with Steve, who had size 14 feet, and with my size 11 foot, we easily had the biggest feet there. We got the second highest number of crates there – 17 crates, just one behind the winners, but they had much smaller feet, so I think we won on a technicality!

At this point I was getting drunk, or at least tipsy, most nights because I couldn't think of a reason not to. This meant that I was not in what you would call a good state of mind. However, with that being said, I got invited to talk at another conference for Real Life Options, my care provider, at where else but the place people know most for making good whiskey. Obviously, I'm talking about Scotland!

Do I tell you about getting lost in Edinburgh? I should probably tell you about the speech and how it went, but I think I will tell you about the drive up to Scotland first. So, I was going with one of my support workers from my apartment building that I lived in, and to say it was an uncomfortable trip up would be an understatement. The person I was going with, although he was a very good driver, had never driven an automatic car before. If you looked into the car from outside or from another car, you would have thought we were really big heavy metal fans because Simon, the person who was driving me up there, hadn't got a hang of the brake, so it looked like we were head banging. At one point, I put some Metallica on for a laugh, but I found it fun so I can't complain too much, and it was an experience, so it's a good story. The reason I was going up with Simon was that he is helping me to plan my next big adventure, but I will tell you about that in a minute.

So, I was talking about the conference I was asked to speak at. I think the speech went well. I was one of the last ones to talk so there was a bit of pressure, but as always, I was just pressing play on my iPad and letting that do the talking. We actually got lost in Edinburgh. I thought that while being in Scotland, I had to go to a whiskey distillery, and I found a new distillery that had just opened. And that was the problem – because it had only just opened no one had heard of it. Luckily, we had arrived in Edinburgh about three hours early and it was a miserable day, and by that, I mean it was raining pretty much all day. So, there we were in the middle of Edinburgh, a guy in a wheelchair and a little balding man, both not having a clue where we were or where we were going. We had to stop every two minutes and ask a local if they had any idea where the place was that we were looking for. But on the other hand, we did get to see a lot of Edinburgh. In fact, I rather enjoyed getting lost anyway.

We finally found the distillery and it turned out to be a really good tour. It was the first whiskey distillery in Edinburgh for 100 years and the leader of the tour explained why, but I'm not going to bore you with that. Another thing that he said annoyed me a bit – he said that whiskey basically was boiled beer, and whilst that is somewhat true, it's so much more than that. I could have had a full-blown argument about it, but I was tired, and my speech isn't good when I'm tired so we probably would have been there all day. So, I decided just to bite my tongue and agree with him. But now, some of the staff at my apartment building have started saying it, and my usual response is to just smile while sticking my middle finger up. I've learned it's no use getting annoyed because it's sort of become a joke.

Lost in Edinburgh - finding a distillery!

Anyway, I said I would tell you what I am trying to plan for my next challenge. It's something I've been saying I wanted to do for a while, but I never really thought I would find someone who was mad enough to go along with it and help me to set up. At the last Dystonia Conference, I bumped into an old friend, and I think she's one of those people who when someone says you can't do something, she says, "why not?" and then she tries to find a way. In other words, she's a kindred spirit, similar to me. I should probably tell you about this mad idea. With my friend, Kyrby, we are planning to do Land's End to John O'Groats, in other words, the bottom of England to the top of Scotland on our Frame Runners! Unfortunately, my body has decided to become more dystonic at the moment, but I've never let that stop me from doing something I've set my mind to. No matter how painful or difficult it will be, I will do it. I'm stubborn like that.

I'm about up to date... a few other things have happened, but as I said before, my memory isn't great. And I don't really know how to end because obviously I'm not dead yet and plan to do more things with my life. But I would like to say thank you to all the people that have helped me over the years, especially my amazing friends and family who have helped me to achieve so much over the years. Even if you've just said 'Hi', thank you. And a massive thank you to the staff member that helped me to write this book.

In fact, a massive thank you to everyone who has helped me over the years; I wouldn't have been able to do half of the things that I've done over my life without you so thanks once again.

Some of the stories that I've mentioned perhaps didn't happen in the order that I referred to them, so I have included a list of the awards and achievements that I've been given and I have done over the years.

Sadly, I have been pushed to see reality and have finally accepted that I won't be able to continue with my plans to complete the Land's End to John o Groats trip I was planning, with my body the way it is at the moment. In other news though, I've been asked to help set up a Frame Running group with my friend Tully, who is already a very successful swimmer with quite a few medals in the Paralympics and other high-profile competitions. I'm still going to strive to do the impossible or mad things I do, it's just right now I am looking for new challenges. I've got a few ideas but I'm not going to tell you what they are, but this isn't the last you'll be seeing of mad Matt!

And that's the end of my story – not in that way – I'm not dying or anything but that's the end of the interesting stuff that has happened in my life so far. I hope you have enjoyed it and that in some ways I've inspired you to do great things, just like I've been able to do great things.

Don't judge a book by its cover and always remember – whatever you feel inspired to do or

achieve, it's only impossible if you say it is!
All the best,
Matthew Humphreys

After the Great Birmingham Run – Half
Marathon flexing muscles showing off.

Bendrigg Trust

Scotland: Holyrood Distillery after getting lost in Edingborough

Awards and Achievements

Pingle Sports Evening – Special Recognition for Cycling – 2014

Derby Mercury RC Presented In Recognition of Rickshaw Challenge Ride for Children In Need 2014

Sixth form – Rita Gray Award for Personal Qualities and Determination – 2014

Derby Telegraph Community Champions – Inspirational Youngster Award 2015

Derby Telegraph Disabled Sports Person of the Year – 2017

Sixth form –Maggie Gorman Prize – 2018

MyCollege – Hucknall Rotary Club – Sports Person of the Year 2018

North West Leicestershire Disabled Sports Person of the Year 2022

Achievements or Medals

Rickshaw Challenge – for Children in Need – 2014

Denmark – Race Runners Cup – 2015

CPISRA World Games – 2015

Denmark – Open European Championships – 2016

Denmark – CPISRA World RaceRunning Championships – 2017

Sant Cugat – Barcelona – CPISRA World Games – 2018

Derby 10k – 2018

Manchester Half Marathon – 2019

Silverston Half Marathon – 2019

Stafford Half Marathon – 2020

Derby Half Marathon – 2020

Great North Re-Imagined (virtual) – 2020

London Marathon 40th Virtual – 2020

Limelight London 10K – 2021

London Marathon – 2021

Great North Run – 2022

Holme Run – Half Marathon – 2022

Great Birmingham Run – Half Marathon – 2022

Leicestershire Half Marathon – 2022

Great Birmingham Run – 2023

Chase the Sun Prestwold Hall – 10 kilometers – 2023

Winter Warrior Run – Half Marathon – 2024

Matt Humphreys

Made in the USA
Columbia, SC
22 March 2025